Public Transportation

LET'S RIDE THE
SUBWAY!

Elisa Peters

PowerKiDS press

New York

For Yeou-Ching, Jeff, and Tristan

Published in 2015 by The Rosen Publishing Group, Inc.
29 East 21st Street, New York, NY 10010

Copyright © 2015 by The Rosen Publishing Group, Inc.

All rights reserved. No part of this book may be reproduced in any form without permission in writing from the publisher, except by a reviewer.

First Edition

Editor: Amelie von Zumbusch
Photo Research: Katie Stryker
Book Design: Andrew Povolny

Photo Credits: Cover Greg Tucker; p. 5 Jade/Blend Images/Getty Images; p. 6 Huntstock/Thinkstock; p. 9 DEX IMAGE/Getty Images; p. 10 PhotoAlto/Jerome Gorin/Brand X Pictures/Getty Images; p. 13 Brooks Payne/Contributor/Flickr Vision/Getty Images; p. 14 Alex Potemkin/E+/Getty Images; p. 17 Philip Lange/Shutterstock.com; p. 18 Victor Torres/Shutterstock.com; p. 21 Marvin E. Newman/Photographer's Choice/Getty Images; p. 22 Blend Images-Granger Wootz/Brand X Images/Getty Images.

Library of Congress Cataloging-in-Publication Data

Peters, Elisa.
 Let's ride the subway! / by Elisa Peters. — First Edition.
     pages cm. — (Public transportation)
 Includes index.
 ISBN 978-1-4777-6521-0 (library binding) — ISBN 978-1-4777-6532-6 (pbk.) — ISBN 978-1-4777-6516-6 (6-pack)
 1. Subways—Juvenile literature. I. Title.
 HE4211.P468 2015
 388.4'2—dc23

2013048495

Manufactured in the United States of America

CPSIA Compliance Information: Batch #WS14PK4: For Further Information contact Rosen Publishing, New York, New York at 1-800-237-9932

CONTENTS

Subways and Cities   4
Taking the Subway   7
Subway Systems   12
Words to Know   24
Websites   24
Index   24

Big cities have **subways**. They are fun to ride!

Go to the station. Look at the **map**. Figure out which line to take.

Pay your fare. Then go through the **turnstile**.

Wait on the platform. When the train comes, get on. Take a seat.

The subway in Boston is the T.
Its lines are named for colors.

New York City has a big subway system. It is the world's longest one!

London is in England. It has the oldest subway system. It is called the London Underground.

Chicago's L goes outside. "L" is short for "elevated." This means "lifted up."

Washington, DC, has the Metro. You can pay with a SmarTrip card there.

Have you ever been on a subway? What city was it in?

WORDS TO KNOW

map   subway   turnstile

WEBSITES

Due to the changing nature of Internet links, PowerKids Press has developed an online list of websites related to the subject of this book. This site is updated regularly. Please use this link to access the list: www.powerkidslinks.com/putr/sub/

INDEX

C
cities, 4, 23

L
line(s), 7, 12

S
system, 15–16

W
Washington, DC, 20